Read All About Dogs

HOUNDS ON THE TRAIL

Barbara J. Patten

The Rourke Corporation, Inc.
Vero Beach, Florida 32964

6867709

PHOTO CREDITS
Photos courtesy of Corel

Library of Congress Cataloging-in-Publication Data

Patten, Barbara J., 1951-
    Hounds on the trail / by Barbara J. Patten.
       p. cm. — (Read all about dogs)
    Includes index.
    Summary: Illustrations and brief text present various breeds of dogs known for their tracking skills, including the Afghan, Irish Wolfhound, Beagle and Dachshund.
    ISBN 0-86593-459-2
    1. Hounds—Juvenile literature. 2. Tracking dogs—Juvenile literature. [1. Hounds. 2. Dogs.]
I. Title II. Series: Patten, Barbara J., 1951- Read all about dogs.
SF429.H6P37   1996
636.7'53—dc20   96–19942
                                                                     CIP
                                                                      AC

Printed in the USA

TABLE OF CONTENTS

HOT ON THE TRAIL

Hounds live a life of adventure. They hunt wild animals, find lost children, and race across finish lines.

Dogs in the hound group are hunters. Some known as coursing hounds depend on sharp eyesight and speed to catch their prey. Others called tracking hounds use a keen sense of smell to follow the scent of another animal or person.

Let's read all about hounds and share the adventure that makes them special.

These basset hounds look worn out after a big day of hunting.

AFGHANS

Looking like a hound wearing pajamas, the **Afghan** (AF GAN) certainly catches attention.

Long, silky hair sways back and forth as this high-stepping hound walks to and fro.

Once used for hunting gazelles and leopards in the Afghanistan desert, the Afghan today is a well-liked companion dog.

The Afghan's fancy coat needs brushing every day.

BASENJIS

The basenji came from Africa and is sometimes called the "African bush dog."

The **basenji** (buh SEN jee) is an unusual dog. Though it looks like most other dogs, basenjis do not bark; and they wash themselves like cats.

They make a yodeling sound that surprises most first-time owners. Cheerful, patient, and clean, basenjis make terrific pets.

IRISH WOLFHOUNDS

Meet the tallest dog in the world, the **Irish wolfhound** (I rish) (WOOLF HOWND). Many years ago, these friendly giants kept wolves away from their master's sheep. They did the job so well that soon no wolves were left in all of Ireland.

Wolfhounds are huge dogs. They stand almost three feet tall at the shoulder, which is how a dog's height is measured.

Even with a long, powerful tail that can knock over a chair with one wag, Irish wolfhounds make good family pets. They do need lots of space to stretch their long legs, though.

Much too big to hide in the grass, this Irish wolfhound weighs about 200 pounds.

WHIPPETS

Even with the finest care, the whippet looks thin and fragile.

Like many coursing hounds, its lean body is built for speed. Able to reach speeds of 35 miles an hour, the whippet has often been used for dog racing. Anything but fragile, this hardy hound is a natural hunter. Whippets most like to chase rabbits.

They make fine pets. Because whippets were made for running, they need lots of exercise.

Born to run, the whippet has a lean, muscular body.

PHARAOH AND IBIZAN HOUNDS

As hunters, the **Pharaoh** (FAIR o) and **Ibizan** (eh BEE zun) hounds have it all. They are speedy and powerful. Also, these hounds can track by both sight and scent.

Their yellowish eyes and large, straight ears make them stand out from the hound crowd. They track rabbits and hunt even in the dark.

Pharaoh hounds and humans have lived together for thousands of years.

Ibizan hounds stand about 26 inches tall and weigh around 50 pounds.

Tombs of ancient Egyptian pharaohs, or kings, show pictures of dogs looking very much like today's Pharaoh and Ibizan hounds. The Ibizans were often drawn wearing large collars, perhaps hinting at their great strength.

These dogs probably have lived with humans for about 5,000 years. Once mostly hunters, today they are lively companions.

BLOODHOUNDS

Sometimes described as a "dog walking behind a nose," the **bloodhound** (BLUD HOWND) has the keenest sense of smell in all the dog world.

Police often use bloodhounds when searching for lost or hiding people. Bloodhounds can follow a person's scent, or smell, a long way over almost any type of ground.

The bloodhound's name does not mean that it is cruel or eager to see blood. In fact, this hound is likely to be friendly with everyone it tracks down.

The bloodhound has a keener sense of smell than any other dog.

BEAGLES

Nothing makes a **beagle** (BEE gul) happier than a good rabbit chase. A pleasant, high-pitched bark tells that the scent has been picked up and the race is on.

Throughout history, hunters have used beagles for searching out small birds and rabbits.

They are small, sturdy hounds weighing about 30 pounds. Long hanging-down ears frame a sweet face.

Beagles are "people" dogs and favorite family pets. They are just as happy tracking slippers at home as they are hunting rabbits in the fields.

This beagle pup is already thinking about rabbits.

DACHSHUNDS

The **dachshund** (DAHKS hoont) looks like a hot dog with short legs. Its build is perfect for squeezing into holes. Long ago dachshunds did just that as they hunted badgers.

Today, instead of chasing badgers, most dachshunds play in backyards. Now they hunt tennis balls the way they went after badgers and other small animals in the past.

Always ready to play, dachshunds are popular family pets.

BLACK-AND-TAN COONHOUNDS

Looking as though the raccoon got away, this black-and-tan coonhound waits patiently.

To hunt raccoons, a dog must be able to pick up a scent and track it in the dark. The **black-and-tan coonhound** (BLAK und TAN) (KOON HOWND) is up to the job.

When the raccoon runs up a tree to get out of danger, the coonhound stands under it and howls.

IS A HOUND FOR YOU?

With nose to the ground or legs flying across the field, a hound may seem like the perfect **canine** (KAY nyn) for you. What fun it would be to explore new places with your dog trotting at your side.

Hounds need lots of exercise to stay happy and healthy. All dogs need clean water, good food, medical care, and a warm, safe place to sleep.

Owning a dog means taking care of it every day—even when you don't want to. Most hound owners will tell you that it's a job worth doing right.

Dachshunds come in two sizes, and some have long or wiry coats.

GLOSSARY

Afghan (AF GAN) — a big, thin hunting dog with long, thick hair and droopy ears

basenji (buh SEN jee) — a dog with a short, smooth reddish coat and without a bark

beagle (BEE gul) — a small hound with short legs, droopy ears, and a smooth coat

black and tan coonhound (BLAK und TAN) (KOON HOWND) — a smooth-coated dog used to hunt raccoons

bloodhound (BLUD HOWND) — a scent-tracking dog with sagging jaws and droopy ears

canine (KAY nyn) — of or about dogs; like a dog

dachshund (DAHKS hoont) — a little dog with short hair and very short legs

Ibizan (eh BEE zun) — a swift, thin, shorthaired hound

Irish wolfhound (I rish) (WOOLF HOWND) — large, strong dog with rough, shaggy coat

Pharaoh (FAIR o) — a sleek, fast hunting dog with glossy coat

The unusual beauty of the Afghan hound is admired by many people.

INDEX